KID CHEMISTRY LAB

UNDERSTANDING CHEMICAL REACTIONS

Jessica Rusick

Checkerboard
Library

An Imprint of Abdo Publishing
abdobooks.com

ABDOBOOKS.COM

Published by Abdo Publishing, a division of ABDO, PO Box 398166, Minneapolis, Minnesota 55439.
Copyright © 2023 by Abdo Consulting Group, Inc. International copyrights reserved in all countries.
No part of this book may be reproduced in any form without written permission from the publisher.
Checkerboard Library™ is a trademark and logo of Abdo Publishing.

Printed in the United States of America, North Mankato, Minnesota
052022
092022

Design and Production: Kelly Doudna, Mighty Media, Inc.
Editor: Liz Salzmann
Cover Photograph: HappyKids/iStockphoto
Interior Photographs: adamkaz/iStockphoto, p. 21; busypix/iStockphoto, p. 5; Dream79/Shutterstock Images, p. 9; feawt/Shutterstock Images, p. 7; julie deshaies/Shutterstock Images, p. 17; Mighty Media, Inc., pp. 26, 27, 28, 29; MLIN/Shutterstock Images, p. 11; Monkey Business Images/Shutterstock Images, pp. 12–13; monkeybusinessimages/iStockphoto, p. 23; SelectStock/iStockphoto, p. 25; udaix/Shutterstock Images, p. 19; Wikimedia Commons, p. 15

Library of Congress Control Number: 2021953167

Publisher's Cataloging-in-Publication Data
Names: Rusick, Jessica, author.
Title: Understanding chemical reactions / by Jessica Rusick.
Description: Minneapolis, Minnesota : Abdo Publishing, 2023 | Series: Kid chemistry lab | Includes online resources and index.
Identifiers: ISBN 9781532199035 (lib. bdg.) | ISBN 9781098272968 (ebook)
Subjects: LCSH: Chemistry--Juvenile literature. | Chemical reactions--Juvenile literature. | Mechanically induced chemical reactions--Juvenile literature. | Science projects--Juvenile literature.
Classification: DDC 540--dc23

CONTENTS

WHAT ARE CHEMICAL REACTIONS?

Have you ever baked a cake or washed your hands with soap? If so, you have seen a chemical reaction! Chemical reactions are important parts of everyday life. They explain why wood burns and how your body **digests** food.

Chemical reactions cause substances to change into different substances. The original substances in a reaction are called reactants. The new substances are called products. Products and reactants are often very different from each other.

For example, a chemical reaction occurs when you mix vinegar and baking soda. These two substances are the reactants. One product of the reaction is water. Another product is **carbon dioxide** gas.

A common science project is to make a volcano with vinegar and baking soda inside it. The reaction causes bubbles to flow out like lava.

BONDS & ENERGY

Everything is made of matter. All matter is made of small pieces called atoms. Atoms bond to form molecules. During a chemical reaction, the bonds between atoms rearrange. Atoms may break apart from each other. Or they may bond with other atoms.

All chemical reactions need energy to happen. This energy can be in the form of heat, light, or electricity. The energy breaks the bonds between reactants. Energy is also released when new products form.

Reactions are either endothermic or exothermic. Endothermic reactions **absorb** more energy than they release. Because of this, substances in the reaction often feel cold. Exothermic reactions release more energy than they absorb, so they create heat. A very quick exothermic reaction can cause an explosion.

A fireworks display is made up of many exothermic reactions.

PHYSICAL CHANGES

Chemical reactions cause chemical changes that produce different substances. Matter can also go through physical changes. Unlike chemical changes, physical changes only affect what a substance looks like. They do not change what a substance is.

An ice cube melting into water is a physical change. Although they look different, ice cubes and water are both made of water molecules. Melting does not cause any new substances to form. So, it is not a chemical reaction.

It can sometimes be hard to tell a chemical change from a physical change. Both can cause substances to change color or temperature or to produce bubbles. The best way to tell a chemical change from a physical one is to look for new substances.

Melting ice cubes
is an endothermic
reaction. The ice
absorbs heat from
the drink. This melts
the ice and makes
the drink colder.

TYPES OF REACTIONS

There are several types of chemical reactions. One is a **synthesis** reaction. This is when two or more substances combine to form a new substance. Table salt is the result of a synthesis reaction. It forms when **sodium** combines with **chlorine**.

Another type of reaction is a **decomposition** reaction. This is when a substance breaks apart into different, simpler substances. **Hydrogen** peroxide is used to clean cuts and surfaces. Over time, it naturally breaks down into water and oxygen.

Rusting is a synthesis reaction. The scientific name for rust is iron oxide. ▶
Iron oxide forms when iron is exposed to water and oxygen.

A third type of reaction is **combustion**, or burning. In a combustion reaction, a heated reactant combines with oxygen. This produces **carbon dioxide**, water, heat, and light.

Methane gas is found underground and in many other places. When heated, it combusts. Power companies mix methane with other substances to form natural gas. Many home furnaces, water heaters, and stoves burn natural gas.

Digesting food is a decomposition reaction. Your body breaks down the substances in your food. This creates the nutrients your body uses to stay healthy.

ACIDS & BASES

Most substances are either acids or bases. Vinegar is an acid. So is lemon juice. Baking soda is a base. Acidic foods usually taste sour. Basic foods usually taste bitter. Bases also feel slippery in water.

Scientists use the pH scale to measure how acidic or basic a substance is. The scale goes from 0 to 14. Substances measuring less than 7 are acidic. Substances measuring more than 7 are basic. Substances that measure exactly 7 are **neutral**.

When an acid and a base mix, it causes an acid-base reaction. This is a type of chemical reaction. Acid-base reactions produce water and sometimes gas. They also produce chemical **compounds** known as salts.

Danish chemist
Søren Peder Lauritz
Sørensen introduced
the idea of pH in 1909.

CHEMICAL EQUATIONS

Chemical reactions are shown with chemical **equations**. The reactants are on the left side of the equation. The products are on the right side. Letters stand for different types of atoms or molecules. Numbers show how many atoms or molecules there are.

There are currently 118 known chemical elements. The letter symbols for the elements are listed in the periodic table of the elements. The table also includes other information about each element.

A **hydrogen** molecule contains two hydrogen atoms. In chemical equations, it is written as H_2. An oxygen molecule contains two oxygen atoms. It is written as O_2. Oxygen and hydrogen molecules react to form water. The chemical equation for this reaction is $2H_2 + O_2 \rightarrow 2H_2O$.

PERIODIC TABLE OF THE ELEMENTS

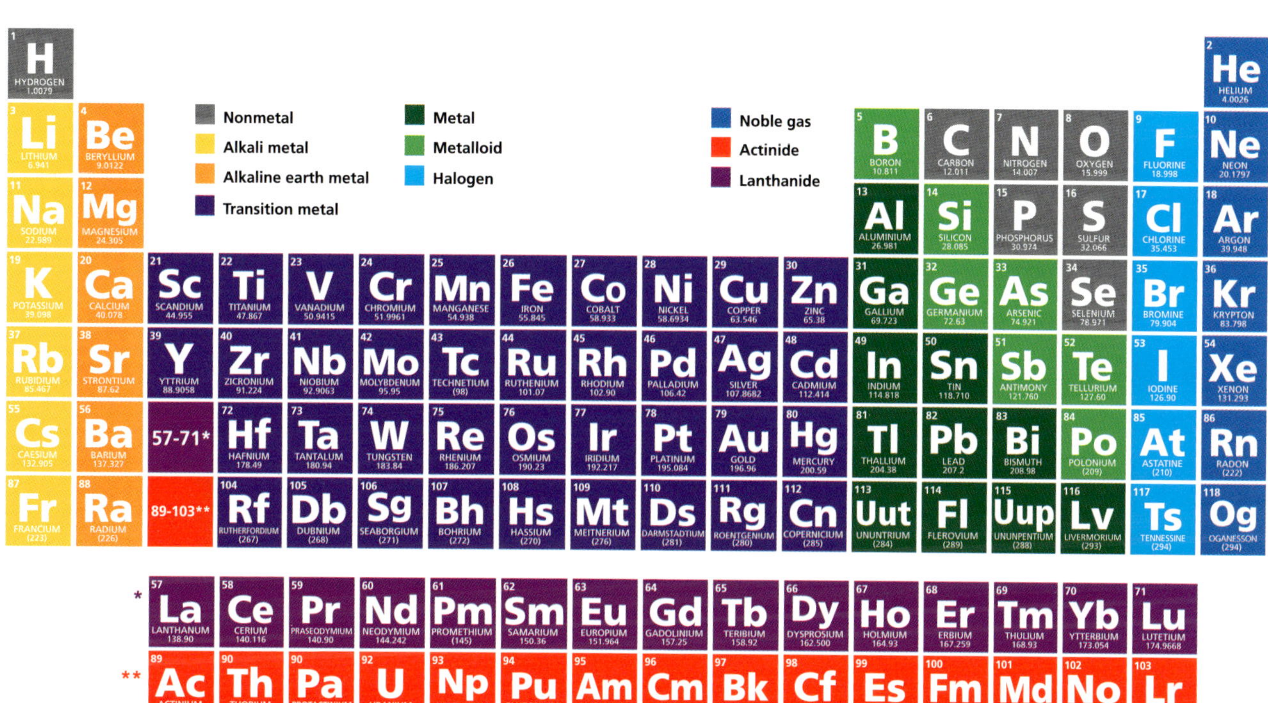

The periodic table is often shown with
each type of element a different color.

There is a *2* in front of H_2 because two **hydrogen** molecules are needed for the reaction. Only one oxygen molecule is needed. The two hydrogen molecules and the oxygen molecule react to form two water molecules. Each water molecule contains two hydrogen atoms connected to one oxygen atom.

Why isn't the chemical **equation** $H_2 + O_2 \rightarrow H_2O$? Because atoms can't be created or destroyed in a chemical reaction. They can only be rearranged. So, each side of an equation must contain the same number and types of atoms.

In the equation on page 16, there are four hydrogen atoms and two oxygen atoms on both sides. So, the equation is balanced. The above equation has two oxygen atoms in the reactants. But it only has one in the products. So, the equation is unbalanced.

CREATING WATER

In a chemical reaction equation, both sides have the same number and type of atoms.

$$2H_2 + O_2 \rightarrow 2H_2O$$

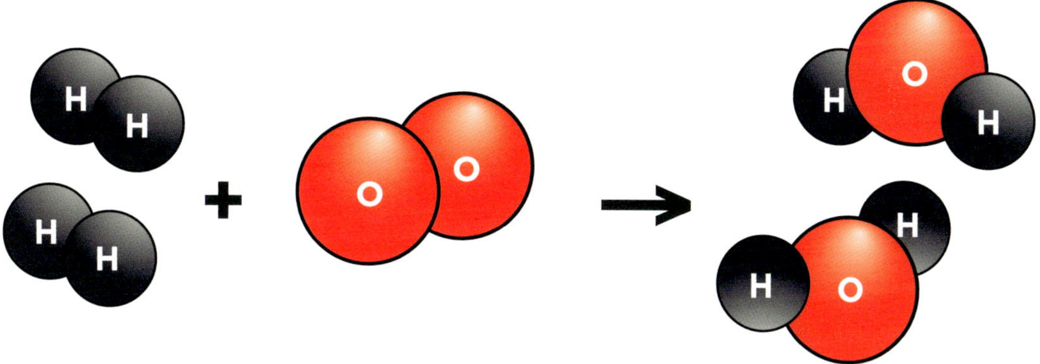

TWO HYDROGEN MOLECULES

They each have two hydrogen atoms.

ONE OXYGEN MOLECULE

It has two oxygen atoms.

TWO WATER MOLECULES

They each have two hydrogen atoms and one oxygen atom.

REACTION RATE

Some reactions, such as explosions, happen quickly. Other reactions happen slowly. Rusting is an example of a slow reaction. It can take many years for a piece of iron to rust completely.

The speed of a reaction is called a reaction rate. Several factors can affect a reaction rate. One is the amount of reactant. If there is less reactant, it can take a longer time for the reaction to happen.

Adding energy can increase a reaction rate. This is because adding energy makes atoms bounce around and **collide** more. The more often atoms collide, the more likely they are to react. One way to add energy

Glow sticks contain chemicals that react to produce light. If the sticks are heated, the reaction happens faster. This ▶ makes the glow brighter, but it won't last as long.

is by heating up the reactants. Adding pressure can
also increase the speed of the reaction. This is because
pressure pushes atoms closer together, making them
more likely to **collide**.

Another way to change the reaction rate is by adding
a **catalyst** or an **inhibitor**. A catalyst is a substance
that speeds up a chemical reaction. An inhibitor is a
substance that slows a chemical reaction. Catalysts and
inhibitors are not reactants. So, they are not used up
or changed in reactions. They are also not included in
chemical **equations**.

Bikes and other products made with metal often have
a special coating to keep the metal from rusting. ▶
The coating acts as an inhibitor.

THE IMPORTANCE OF CHEMICAL REACTIONS

Many people have helped scientists better understand chemical reactions. In 1803, British scientist John Dalton proposed the atomic **theory** of matter. The theory said that chemical reactions cause atoms to rearrange into new substances.

Dalton's theory helped lay the foundation for much of modern chemistry. It helped scientists understand how and why chemical reactions happen. Today, chemical reactions are used in every aspect of chemistry. They help scientists produce energy, date fossils, and create thousands of everyday products.

Illnesses and diseases are caused by chemical reactions in our bodies. Understanding chemical reactions helps scientists and doctors develop medicines and treat patients.

BLOW-UP BALLOON

WHAT HAPPENS

Vinegar and baking soda react when mixed. This is an acid-base reaction. One product of the reaction is **carbon dioxide** gas. This gas fills the bottle and then the balloon, making the balloon inflate.

MATERIALS

- plastic bottle
- measuring cups & spoons
- vinegar
- balloon
- funnel
- baking soda

STEPS

1 Pour ½ cup of vinegar into the bottle.

2 Use a funnel to put 2 tablespoons of baking soda in the balloon.

3 Fit the balloon opening over the top of the bottle. Be careful not to let any baking soda fall into the bottle yet.

4 Hold the balloon up so the baking soda falls into the bottle. Watch the balloon inflate!

THE SCIENTIFIC METHOD

Want to experiment like a real chemist? Follow the scientific method! The scientific method is a process scientists use to answer questions.

1. **Ask a question.** Research your question to learn more about it.

2. **Develop a hypothesis.** This is your best guess about the answer to your question.

3. **Experiment to test your hypothesis.** Record what happens during the experiment.

4. **Review the results of your experiment to draw a conclusion.** Was your hypothesis supported? Why or why not? Share your results with others.

HARDENED MILK

WHAT HAPPENS

Mixing milk and vinegar causes a chemical reaction. Milk contains molecules of a protein called casein. Casein reacts with acid in the vinegar. Adding heat to this reaction causes the casein molecules to break apart and reorganize. This is what forms the moldable lumps!

EXPERIMENT!

Try the project with different types of milk. Or try different acids, such as lemon or lime juice. Do you get the same result?

MATERIALS

- milk
- measuring cups & spoons
- stove or hot plate
- saucepan
- bowl
- white vinegar
- spoon
- strainer
- sink
- paper towels
- markers or paint

STEPS

1 Have an adult heat 1 cup of milk on the stove until it is hot but not boiling.

2 Carefully pour the milk into the bowl.

3 Add 4 teaspoons of vinegar. Stir the vinegar and milk gently for one minute. Lumps should form in the milk.

4 Hold the strainer over the sink. Pour the mixture into the strainer. Gently press the lumps to release more liquid.

5 Place the lumps on a paper towel. Pat them dry with more paper towels to remove more liquid.

6 Press the lumps together to form a ball or other shape.

7 Leave the shape to dry for a few days. Then, color it with markers or paint!

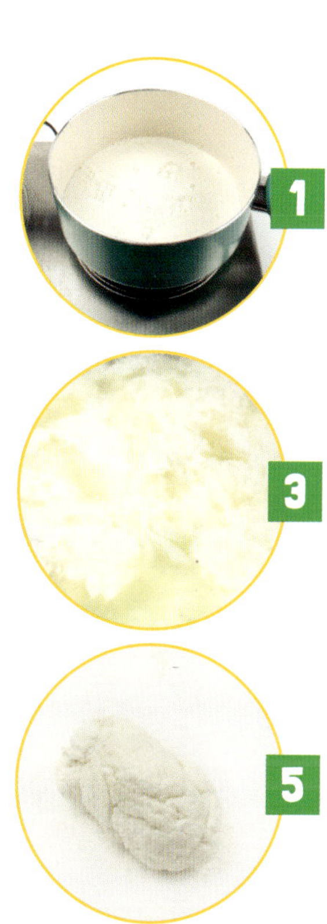

GLOSSARY

absorb—to soak up or take in.

carbon dioxide—a heavy, colorless gas that is released when people and animals breathe out and produced when some fuels are burned.

catalyst—a substance that causes a chemical reaction to happen more quickly.

chlorine (KLOR-een)—a chemical element that under normal conditions is a greenish-yellow gas and has a strong smell.

collide—to come together with force.

combust—to burn. The act or process of burning is combustion.

compound—a chemical or substance that is formed by combining two or more parts or elements.

decomposition—the act or process of breaking down into simpler parts.

digest—to break down food into simpler substances the body can absorb.

equation—a mathematical or chemical statement showing equality between two sides separated by an equal sign or arrow.

hydrogen—the lightest chemical element. It is a gas with no smell or color and catches fire easily.

hypothesis (hye-PAH-thi-sis)—an unproven idea or theory based on known facts that leads to further study.

inhibitor—a substance that slows or interferes with a chemical reaction.

neutral (NOO-truhl)—neither acidic nor basic.

sodium—a soft, waxy, silver-white chemical element. It is found in compounds such as salt and baking soda.

synthesis—the production of a substance by combining other substances through a chemical process.

theory (THEE-uh-ree)—a general rule offered to explain a scientific event.

ONLINE RESOURCES

To learn more about chemical reactions, please visit **abdobooklinks.com** or scan this QR code. These links are routinely monitored and updated to provide the most current information available.

INDEX